Rancho Pancho is riveting theater. It is set partly during the writing and casting for *A Streetcar Named Desire* (titled "Poker Night" at the time). Pancho Rodriguez was the inspiration for the brutish Stanley Kowalski in *Streetcar*, and there are lots of references to the play throughout.

– *San Antonio Express-News*

In Gregg Barrios' new play, *Rancho Pancho*, the playwright takes Rodriguez, who has been a peripheral character (in Williams' life) for the longest time and gives him center stage.

– *New Orleans Times-Picayune*

In *Rancho Pancho*, Barrios creates a three-dimensional Tennessee not seen before. He also gives us a Pancho who is not only as complex as Kowalski, but he shows us that Pancho is in fact him, or vice versa.

– *San Antonio Current*

Playwright Gregg Barrios leaves Tennessee Williams upstaged in his play *Rancho Pancho*. Barrios' intent is not just to revisit a period in the playwright's life but also to revise popular and critical understandings of how his life intersected with Pancho Rodriguez.

– *New Orleans' Gambit Weekly*

Rancho Pancho, an excellent new spin on Tennessee Williams that features his relatively little-known friend Pancho Rodriguez. Barrios spent years researching the relationship between Williams and Rodriguez and it's likely the play will have legs, as they say in the business.

– *D Magazine*

D1225587

RANCHO PANCHO

RANCHO PANCHO

a play by

Gregg Barrios

Foreword by David Kaplan

ଈଓଓଃ

HANSEN PUBLISHING GROUP, LLC

Rancho Pancho copyright © 2009 by Gregg Barrios

Rancho Pancho is published by Hansen Publishing Group, LLC, 302 Ryders Lane, East Brunswick, NJ 08816

16 15 14 13 12 11 10 09   1 2 3 4 5

International Standard Book Number: 978-1-60182-331-1

Book design and typography by Jon Hansen

All rights reserved. Except for brief passages quoted in newspaper, magazine, radio or television reviews, no part of this book may be reproduced in any form or by any means, electronic or mechanical, including photocopying or recording, or by an information storage and retrieval system, without permission in writing from the publisher.

Professionals and amateurs are hereby warned that this material, being fully protected under the Copyright Laws of the United States of America and all other countries of the Berne and Universal Copyright Conventions, is subject to a royalty. All rights including, but not limited to, professional, amateur, recording, motion picture, recitation, lecturing, public reading, radio and television broadcasting, and the rights of translation into foreign languages are expressly reserved. Particular emphasis is placed on the question of readings and all uses of this book by educational institutions, permission for which must be secured from the author's agent, Hansen Publishing Group, LLC.

The worldwide stage performance rights to this play (other than first-class rights) are controlled exclusively by the author. No professional or non-professional performance of the play (excluding first-class professional performance) may be given without obtaining, in advance, written permission from the author's agent and paying the requisite fee. For information about performance rights or any other rights, please contact Jon Hansen c/o Hansen Publishing Group LLC, 302 Ryders Lane, East Brunswick, NJ 08816. (732) 220-1211.

Grateful acknowledgment is made to New Directions for permission to quote from the works of Tennessee Williams and from *A Member of the Wedding*, a play by Carson McCullers. Used by permission of New Directions Publishing Corporation.

Grateful acknowledgement is made for permission to quote from the song, "María Bonita," words and music by Agustín Lara. Used by permission.

Grateful acknowledgment is made to the *Texas Observer* for permission to reprint "The Kindness of Strangers."

Grateful acknowledgement is made to Diane Malone, co-Artistic Director of The Classic Theatre of San Antonio for permission to use her photograph from the San Antonio Production of *Rancho Pancho* for the cover.

Hansen Publishing Group, LLC
302 Ryders Lane
East Brunswick, NJ 08816

1-877-876-4716
http://hansenpublishing.com

This play is dedicated to

Brother Alexis Gonzales, F.S.C.
(1931-2006)

Foreword

An ambiguous relationship between two men has been the subject matter of Western literature since Western literature began: the story of Gilgamesh and Enkidu punched into clay slabs, the story in the Bible of David and Jonathan scratched onto sheepskins, the story in the *Iliad* of Achilles and Patroklus, recited aloud. These are all friendships, of course, heroic ones, mythic ones, and what they don't have to deal with — any of the authors or any of the characters — is the day to day living together: who takes out the garbage, who entertains the other's friends.

There is also a Western tradition of denouncing relationships between two men (or two women) when ambiguity dissolves and love surfaces. As Amiri Baraka (formerly Leroi Jones) pointed out at the Provincetown Tennessee Williams Theater Festival the year before Gregg Barrios' play, *Rancho Pancho,* performed there: same-sex relations are innately an assault on traditional roles and power structures. Sedition, too, has an aesthetic, and the halo of the outlaw lends glamour, and sometimes humor, to the depictions of relations between men in the work of Jean Genet, John Rechy, and Joe Orton, but again, domesticity, except ironically, is not part of their stories, anymore than Bonnie and Clyde's home life or Ma Barker's home cooking. Outlaw status, too, fuels the eruptions of gas from bigots claiming a divine revelation that same sex relations are unavoidably doomed: domesticity among the damned an aberration of an aberration.

Then there is romance — the camaraderie of the road, or the hotel room — celebrated by Walt Whitman on the battle-field or the swimming hole, or in Michelangelo's sonnets, or Shakespeare's for that matter, or Baudelaire's — but there is no poem by any of these writers about painting the house and cleaning the brushes. The one grand exception I can think of, though I'm sure there are others, is Herman Melville who, in *Moby Dick*, shows us two men in bed not making love, but working out who hogs the covers.

The domestic life of two men living together has had to wait — and a long time — to become background matter, not to mention subject matter. A writer as subversive, as romantic, as mythical, and as honest as Tennessee Williams chose not to write (for public performance) about his own day-to-day experiences. In his publicly produced plays, the closest Williams got to his own home life are the dead and gone "pair of old maids" Peter Occello and Jack Straw who haunt the bedroom of *Cat on a Hot Tin Roof* – but we don't see them. We see the ambiguities of Maggie and Brick.

Why didn't Williams — certainly open about his sexuality among his friends and professional colleagues — write about domesticity between men? For one thing, it was against the law. You couldn't get a license, not in New York or in London, to show such plays onstage. That's the least of the probable consequences. Fines, theater-closings, arrest, blacklists and exile would have followed any open discussion of homosexuality. Williams did have the option of brave career suicide, but his way was to infiltrate the Broadway stage and Hollywood — which he did. These habits of the saboteur — informed by the traditions of Southern discretion and Southern backstabbing — were his survival tactics. To save himself and other people he needed to be discreet about himself and other people. When it came time to write his *Memoirs*, Williams, had good stories to tell about Pancho Rodriguez — with whom he lived tempestuously for two years, and Williams told those stories — but even in 1975, he felt concerned for Pancho's reputation and disguised the name as Santo, and omitted to say that they still kept in touch.

So it fell to Gregg Barrios to tell the story of Pancho and Tennessee. It hasn't, so far, appeared in a biography of Williams. In the afterword to the play Barrios writes of his discovery and research. The beautiful appropriateness of having the story first told onstage should be noted.

Note too, what Barrios has done in *Rancho Pancho* is present real people in a specific situation that can be configured in a number of ways: older man/younger man (Williams was 35, Pancho 25), acclaimed man/undervalued man (*Glass Menagerie* was playing on Broadway, Pancho was working in a department store), Anglo/Chicano (in race conscious America). A visit by a third person, the writer Carson McCullers, herself a constellation of contradictions, brings out the latent aspects of the men's relationship — jealousy, competition, partnership. Another third wheel, the director Margo Jones, arrives in the second act to pass on the opinions of the outside world and ruin whatever chances the two men had to fuse their differences.

Barrios himself intrudes on the Williams/Rodriguez relationship by dramatizing that the greatest of American playwrights wove his cloth of dreams with threads picked up south of the border. With what's presented onstage we can see for ourselves how that transference of heritage and knowledge happens. That it is personal, always, if it is true. That the appropriator acts out of love, admiration, appreciation, personal need — and is met with a tangle of responses: pride, resentment, short-sighted possessiveness, and pain. Barrios makes it clear that great artists don't borrow, they steal. What they take they make their own.

What Barrios has stolen is the lives of real people — and he has made of those lives his own living thing: a play that doesn't just happen to be about two men living together, but a play in which the details of two men living together are elevated, made significant — intermittently romantic, mythic and glamorously perverse. Bravo!

There are other such stories to be told: Gertrude Stein and Alice B. Toklas, Mrs. Annie Fields and Sarah Orne Jewett (look them up), Tennessee Williams and Frank Merlo who lived together for thirteen years. Wait, Barrios is already at work on that one.

David Kaplan, Curator
Provincetown Tennessee Williams Theater Festival

Acknowledgements

The author wishes to thank the following for their contributions to the development and success of *Rancho Pancho*. This work would not have been possible without you.

All the folks at the Tennessee Williams Literary Festival in New Orleans; Fred Todd for his generous support; David Kaplan for his time and talent; the Provincetown Tennessee Williams Festival; Johnny Rodriguez for his insights into Tennessee Williams and his brother Pancho; the Church Theater and Diane Malone for her peerless imagining of the play; the Classic Theatre of San Antonio for moving the play to its next level; the Jump-Start Performance Company; Joe De Salvo at the Faulkner House Books; the Guadalupe Cultural Arts Center for the Gateway Ford Foundation Grant; Olivia Revueltas for providing the original music; Virginia Spencer Carr for insights into Carson and Pancho; Sandra Cisneros for the play's title; Donald Windham for the Pennyland recordings; Walter Starcke for Tennessee's laugh; Jon and Jody Hansen, the most thoughtful publishers in the business; Deborah Martin for her thoughtful criticism; and especially the actors in the numerous workshops and readings that ultimately led to the finished script.

Production History

This text is based on the production of *Rancho Pancho* that opened at Jump-Start Performance Co., San Antonio, TX, on September 6, 2008, produced by The Classic Theatre of San Antonio in association with Jump-Start Performance Co. It was directed by Diane Malone, the set design and costume design were by Diane Malone, the lighting design was by Felice Garcia and the sound design was by Rick Malone. The production stage manager was Annella Keys. The cast was as follows:

RICK FREDERICK	TENNESSEE
BENNY BRISENO	PANCHO
ANNA GANGAI	CARSON
ANNELLA KEYS	MARGO

Rancho Pancho was subsequently produced by The Classic Theatre of San Antonio at the Fisherman's Wharf Theater in Provincetown, MA as part of the Provincetown Tennessee Williams Theater Festival on September 27, 2008. The same cast and crew from the San Antonio production participated.

RANCHO PANCHO

Influence is simply transference of personality, a mode of giving away what is most precious to one's self, and its exercise produces a sense, and, it may be, a reality of loss. Every disciple takes away something from his master.

- Oscar Wilde, *The Portrait of Mr. W. H.*

Act One

SCENE ONE

NANTUCKET. RANCHO PANCHO. LATE AFTERNOON.
SUMMER 1946.

Interior of a grey dilapidated two story house. The set is a living room with an adjoining kitchen.

PANCHO/CARSON/TENN (*O.S.*): "...Alla en el Rancho Grande, alla donde vivia..."

Enter TENN, PANCHO, and CARSON. PANCHO strums a guitar to a crescendo.

PANCHO: Welcome to Nantucket, home of sperm whales, Moby Dick and sand crabs.

Nuestra casa es su casa, Señorita McCullers.

TENN: Bienvenida a Rancho Pancho.

CARSON: Pancho?

TENN: It's named after the man of the house.

PANCHO: My baptismal name is Amado Francisco Rodriguez, but early on my twin brother and I were known as Pancho and Juancho.

You'd think our parents would have baptized us with proper Latin names: Romulus and Remus or even Mark Anthony and Julius Caesar.

No such luck. They named us after second-rate saints.

Call me Pancho for lack of a better name.

TENN: Just like the Mexican revolutionary, Pancho Villa.

Abajo con los gringos!

CARSON: How delightful.

Sound of radio music fills the room.

PANCHO: The electricity is back on. We had a terrible tormenta last night.

CARSON: Tormenta?

TENN: Just a freak storm.

CARSON: Torment? Right?

PANCHO: The wind blew out some window panes upstairs.

But I shouldn't complain. Everything in Nantucket is a shade of gray.

Carson, you will sleep in our bed upstairs, and we'll share the sofa.

Our desire, señorita, is to make your stay a gay and lively one.

CARSON: Oh, I'd be fine on the sofa.

PANCHO: Did you recognize us right away?

CARSON: I was going to ask the same question.

PANCHO: When Tenn said he had invited you to spend a few weeks, I couldn't believe it.

And yes, I had an idea of what you look like. I bought a copy of *The Heart is a Lonely Hunter* – which would make a great title for my own story some day.

When I saw your photograph on the book jacket, I couldn't believe someone your age – our age wrote it, until I noticed a cigarette in your right hand (laughs).

CARSON: Given to vices at an early age. I'd be honored to sign it, Pancho. You are quite a caballero.

TENN: (*from kitchen*) Carson, since we're both from Columbus, Mississippi, I thought I'd spot you like a hound dog in heat – although I don't recollect mother mentioning your family.

Wearing that baseball cap and man's shirt, I admit fooled me.

I had happily imagined a college boy out cruising for a ménage à trois.

CARSON: It's Georgia. I was born in Columbus, Georgia.

And I certainly wish you'd bring those drinks across that state line to Rancho Pancho.

Or do we need a ferry to cross over?

TENN: (*carrying a drink tray*) Now, the whiskey sour mash is for our distinguished guest, the scotch and soda for Pancho, and the usual for me.

CARSON: And what might that be, dear friend?

TENN: A double, of course.

CARSON: This drink is superb, how did you know I drank whiskey?

TENN: Mercy. I reckon I can tell what my *tocayo* drinks.

PANCHO: *Tocayo* is Spanish for namesake. Since you were both born in a town with the same name, it practically makes you twins.

(*to Carson*) Tenn is trying to practice his Spanish.

TENN: I may not remember your home state, young lady, but I do remember what a person drinks. A toast.

CARSON: Oh yes, a toast.

May the conviviality of this moment, allow two humble writers to embark on an exciting voyage of friendship, admiration and...

(*to Pancho*)...debauchery.

PANCHO moves into the kitchen, searching through the liquor cabinet.

TENN: Is something wrong, Pancho?

PANCHO: I'm looking for my mescal. I want to offer our guest another toast.

Ah, here it is.

He returns to the living room.

PANCHO: Un brindis. An old Mexican toast: To health and wealth, more power to your elbow, and many secret love affairs and time to enjoy them.

PANCHO entwines his arm with the others in typical Mexican fashion as they down the liquor.

CARSON: May this be the start of a beautiful friendship.

PANCHO: 1941. Humphrey Bogart and Claude Rains. The final line of *Casablanca*.

They burst out laughing, feeling the drinks.

PANCHO moves between them on the sofa.

CARSON: Oh my, Pancho, this is so unusual. What is it?

TENN: (*whispering to Carson*) Juice from the maguey cactus. The poor man's tequila.

PANCHO: Mescal. The sacred drink of my ancestors. Ajua!

CARSON: It's delicious and so intoxicating. I like a strong drink.

> *PANCHO holds the bottle for inspection.*

> Oh my, is that a worm at the bottom?

TENN: It looks like a boll weevil larva, but Mexicans say it's an aphrodisiac.

PANCHO: (*sliding closer to Carson*) It will make you howl at the moon tonight, Señorita Carson.

CARSON: How romantic. And I hope we get good and – drunker.

TENN: I'll definitely drink to that.

CARSON: I like your nickname Pancho better than Amado Francisco Rodriguez. It's more masculine. Amado echoes Amanda.

PANCHO: And may I call you something more feminine than Carson, which sounds like a tightwad banker's name?

> Manflora, perhaps?

TENN: (*taken aback*) Pancho, isn't that Spanish for dyke?

CARSON: (*holding Pancho's face*) Why that's a lovely name. Flora. Although I'm not much of a vamp, actually I'm rather shy. That's why I disguised myself as a boy.

> Haven't you ever done that? Pretend to be someone you're not?

PANCHO: (*taking her hand*) Actually I do it all the time.

CARSON: I swear your eyes have changed colors in this light. Or am I already feeling the effects of the mescal – south of the border?

> Tenn, aren't Pancho's eyes greener in this light?

TENN: And his skin seems lighter.

CARSON: runs her fingers through PANCHO's hair as TENN lets his hands roam.

TENN: This is a new development. Those exercises are working.

PANCHO turns toward TENN who tries to French him but finds CARSON instead. Embarrassed, TENN pecks PANCHO on the cheek.

PANCHO: I already feel that this summer is going to be a grand adventure for all of us. Verdad?

PANCHO puts his arms around TENN and CARSON.

BLACKOUT.

ഇരിക്ക

SCENE TWO

RANCHO PANCHO. THE NEXT NIGHT.

PANCHO sits at the kitchen table reading in his undershorts and an athletic shirt.

PANCHO: (*reading*) "I can't stand this existence – this kitchen – any longer! I will hop a train and go to New York, or hitch rides to Hollywood. Or join the Merchant Marines and run away to sea."

Boy, Frankie is so like me, it scares me. Even her name echoes mine.

He evokes their names as if casting a spell.

"Frankie – Frank – Francis – Francisco."

CARSON enters – a ghostly apparition in a shimmering white slip.

PANCHO: Carson?

CARSON: (*dazed*) What – where am I?

PANCHO: (*startled*) You're here. In Rancho Pancho. Are you alright?

CARSON: (*waking up*) Oh, thank goodness.

> Whenever I lay my body down in a new place, I sleepwalk.

> I am so afraid of the dark – that my body automatically gravitates toward any form of light.

> Once I nearly walked off a pier – drawn to the beam of a distant lighthouse.

> What are you doing at this ungodly hour? Are you afraid of the dark, too?

PANCHO: Nothing like that. Actually, you caught me red-handed. I was reading your novel, *The Member of the Wedding.* I waited until Tenn was asleep to borrow his copy.

> I didn't mean to disturb your rest.

CARSON: Oh, no. But why read it in the middle of the night?

PANCHO: I want to finish it before dawn. After hearing you and Tenn discussing it this afternoon, I felt stupid not having anything to contribute.

CARSON: Gracias, Pancho.

> Do you read Tenn's work as diligently?

PANCHO: No, but only because he's a playwright – not a real writer like yourself – or Miss Kathleen Winsor. Her *Forever Amber* was my favorite in senior high.

> Everyone laughed at me for choosing a woman's book for my research paper.

> Still, I was the only one to get an A+ on my report.

CARSON: Dear Pancho, you are most simpatico.

I'm almost jealous of Tenn for having found such a perfect partner – his other half, his other self.

That's a theory Plato set forth in his *Symposium*, but I haven't fully grasped its profundity – even after many a midnight reading.

They laugh.

PANCHO: I wish what you say about Tenn and me was true.

Sometimes I feel like Frankie in your novel, a grown-up inside, but treated like a child to be humored.

In grade school, our teacher made those with Spanish names change them into their American equivalent. My Francisco became Frank, and my nickname Pancho became Frankie.

When I asked why girls named Panchita became Frankie too, our red-headed teacher who looked like Agnes Moorehead explained that English didn't discriminate gender.

CARSON: Well, perhaps, but English does discriminate by color, race and in so many other ugly ways.

PANCHO: Carson, what happens after the novel ends? Does Frankie find happiness with her friend Mary Littlejohn?

I guess I shouldn't ask such personal questions.

CARSON: Pancho! What an intelligent response.

The answer lies in Frankie's – Panchita's – narration at the end.

As for her love life, I believe she's experienced life from both sides of the divide.

Like I – we both have. Let me show you.

CARSON moves behind PANCHO.

Her hands on his shoulder, PANCHO and CARSON slowly read from the book.

CARSON: (*reading*) "We had a letter from Jarvis and Janice. Jarvis is with the Occupation Forces in Germany and they took a vacation trip to Luxembourg."

PANCHO: (*reading*) "Don't you think that's a lovely name?"

CARSON/PANCHO: (*reading together*) "Mary and I will most likely pass through Luxembourg when we are going around the world together."

After what seems an eternity, PANCHO stands. There is a look of satisfaction as he faces CARSON.

LIGHT FADES.

ಬಿೞ

SCENE THREE

RANCHO PANCHO. TWO DAYS LATER.

CARSON and TENN sit at opposite ends of the kitchen table.

They wile away the time playing FISH.

CARSON: I don't know what could be taking him so long.

TENN: It's not as if he were putting on his clothes but taking them off.

CARSON: I need a 9.

TENN: Go Fish.

CARSON: That woman at the party last night, the Baroness. I am smitten by her beauty and her regal quality – just like Katherine Anne.

TENN: Porter?

CARSON: Ah. Yes. She is the most beautiful woman I ever met. I sat outside her door at Yadoo and howled like a bitch in heat.

11

TENN: My, my. Did she open the door?

CARSON: You're damned right. Only to step over me and complain to the director that I was stalking her.

(*as Porter*) "Is that a boy or a girl?" She said.

Do you have a queen?

TENN: One queen coming up.

Do you have a Jack of Hearts?

CARSON: Speaking of Jacks. Where did you meet Pancho? Mexico?

TENN: I was returning from a heavenly sojourn in Mexico. And like Hart Crane, I must have been born Mexican in another life.

But once on this side, my manuscripts were confiscated at the border crossing in Eagle Pass. The war was still raging, so perhaps they found my prose homoerotic, even...

(*sotto voce*)...subversive.

I had to wait for days until they were released.

To wile the time away, I stumbled into an all-night cantina. The handsome Mexican behind the bar? Pancho.

I told him my sad story. We hit it off. Turned out that his father was a U.S. Border customs agent.

Pancho spoke on my behalf and saved my literary hide.

CARSON: I would have proposed on the spot. What a sweetheart.

TENN: Well, I later met his family and invited him to be my guest in New Orleans. But like strangers passing in the dead of night, I lost track of him until a year ago...

CARSON: ...That's hard to imagine. He's so tall, so manly. I find him very attractive.

TENN: He had volunteered for the Army and served in the South Pacific, right in the thick of it, but then was let out without an honorable discharge simply because he had a spell of confusion and talked too trustingly to an officer about it.

He returned with nothing to show for what he went through, and none of his GI compensations, which is an outrage.

CARSON: Poor baby boy. My husband Reeves was wounded in the War, and it was hell for him to just get his disability discharge.

Pancho and Reeves should talk. They seem to have a lot in common. Besides, Reeves needs more diversion. Maybe a trip here would do him – us some good.

TENN: Anyway, baby, I used to go swimming every day at the New Orleans Athletic Club. Gentlemen only!

CARSON: I'll get us a drink for this. Go on.

CARSON moves to the portable bar and mixes the drinks.

TENN: I was sitting at the edge of the pool contemplating a character for my new play.

CARSON: The one you're working on now? *Summer and Smoke*?

TENN: No. It's called "Poker Night." It's about two sisters of the old South and one comes to stay with the other. I'm thinking of setting it in Chicago.

But I was looking for a macho as they say in Mexico for the principal male role. A Mexican.

CARSON hands TENN his drink and sits down.

CARSON: This is getting good.

TENN: I heard this splashing in the water. Someone whispered my name.

I thought I was dreaming. And suddenly as if the goddess Erato had answered my libations … this young god arose from the sea.

CARSON: I've got goose bumps.

TENN: He stood there, dripping wet.

> *PANCHO enters the front door in his swim trunks.*
>
> *PANCHO is returning from an early morning swim. The light from the sun outside etches his body in relief in the open door.*
>
> *TENN and CARSON do not see him.*

TENN: Botticelli's Penis Rising!

PANCHO: As long as you don't call me a wetback, your wish is my command.

TENN: I was speechless. My wish had come true.

PANCHO: Come on in, the water's fine.

> *As PANCHO says these words, he walks into the kitchen, breaking the reverie.*

PANCHO: I thought we were going for a swim?

CARSON: We thought you were still asleep.

TENN: We were finishing a game of Fish. And I just won. The Jack of Hearts.

> *As they head for the door, CARSON retrieves the bottle of Scotch.*

CARSON: Snake oil for our suntan?

> *BLACKOUT.*

ഇൻൽ

SCENE FOUR

RANCHO PANCHO. LATER, THE NEXT AFTERNOON

CARSON and TENN sit at the dining room table. PANCHO is asleep on the sofa.

There are typewriters in front of them and a half-empty bottle of Southern Comfort at the center of the table.

A wind-up Victrola in the corner plays "La Golondrina".

TENN: (*typing in a spurt of energy*) I'm on a roll.

CARSON: I'm in the middle of a scene. I can't stop.

PANCHO rises from the sofa, adjusting to the light.

The recording on the Victrola winds down. No one moves to crank it up. It moans to a stop.

PANCHO: (*startled*) I had a nightmare.

He places a chair between TENN and CARSON, waiting for a pause in their activity.

PANCHO: I was back in Texas. Maybe Mexico. And I was sleeping. Can you imagine? A dream of sleeping.

TENN places a cigarette in a holder.

PANCHO: And for a moment, I thought I was dead because the room was so nice and clean, and the bed had white linen sheets, and I didn't have to share it with my brother or sisters.

And then I realized that I wasn't at home or in my shared bed. I was in a gringo's house or maybe his hotel room.

I knew he was a gringo because he didn't smell like those drunks in a border cantina, who all looked like my father, and who treated me like crap.

All focus on PANCHO as if listening to an Orson Welles radio drama.

PANCHO: I found myself all alone in this room. And I knew it wouldn't work. I knew that as much as I tried to be the best little kept boy, he'd leave me for another – whiter one. And that's when I awoke.

PANCHO moves to the kitchen for a cup of coffee, trying to shake his nightmare.

When he spots a bottle in the bar, he forgoes the coffee.

TENN: Pancho, are you feeling better?

I wanted to ask you about that town across the border from Eagle Pass?

PANCHO: Piedras Negras?

You're rewriting *Summer and Smoke* on the border?

TENN: I've taken Margo Jones' suggestion under advisement. I'm adding a scene with a Mexican family. Margo is planning a production in Dallas in the fall.

CARSON: Margo? The Mexican actress in *Lost Horizons*? She is truly amazing. I saw that film three times.

PANCHO: She's one of my favorites too. Oh, Carson, I didn't know she was Mexican.

TENN: We're talking about Miss Margo Jones, the theater director. Her enthusiasm however often outraces her ability to convince.

Margo and Pancho rarely see eye to eye. I've never understood why.

PANCHO: (*to Carson*) She's rude and bossy. *Es una cabróna.*

TENN: She's a director.

PANCHO: (*to Carson*) She believes that she's the next Mrs. Tennessee Williams. I hate her so much that sometimes I could –

PANCHO smashes an empty liquor bottle against the wall.

CARSON: (*startled*) Oh Pancho, are you hurt?

He's bleeding.

TENN: (*ignoring Carson*) Pancho, apologize for your behavior in front of our guest.

PANCHO kneels in front of CARSON who stands over him, wraps her scarf as a bandage over his hand, then hugs him as a mother an errant child.

CARSON: Can't you see he's sorry and hurt? I know how it feels to be trampled on by a bigger bully.

TENN: Are you okay, Pancho?

PANCHO stands sheepishly, nods and gives Tenn a kiss.

TENN: Now as I was saying, I'm writing a scene in Piedras Negras.

Spell that for me, Pancho.

PANCHO: P-I-E-D-R-A-S   N-E-G-R-A-S.

TENN pecks at his typewriter.

CARSON returns to her work as PANCHO sulks. He reads over TENN's shoulder.

PANCHO: Ah, answered prayers, the coward's way out – especially when your boyfriend's truth fills in the blanks.

Which one is me, and which one my brother Juancho?

TENN: I am doing a scene in Piedras Negras. Neither you or your brother is in the scene.

PANCHO: (*to Carson, who continues writing*) Her first name is Rosa after his loony sister and my sainted mother – and her last name is Gonzalez – our maternal surname.

A Rose by another name is still a Rosa in English or español.

CARSON: Pancho, would you be a sweetheart and get us another bottle.

PANCHO: Yes, Carson. And some ice?

(*in sing-song fashion*) Yellow! Yellow! Yellow!

CARSON: Yellow? Why would you say that?

PANCHO: Yellow is a homonym for *hielo* which means ice in Spanish. And ice is a homonym for eyes.

CARSON: How original. Did you hear that, Tenn?

PANCHO brings in the ice bucket and two liquor bottles.

CARSON: Pancho, you were in the service. Could you help me with some factual information?

PANCHO: (*to Tenn, angrily*) Did you tell her about that?

TENN: No, of course, not. I mentioned that you had been overseas in the South Pacific. Nothing more. Nada.

CARSON: I'm adapting *The Member of the Wedding* into a play. It's kind of like giving birth to the same child twice.

PANCHO: Like having twins?

CARSON: (*excited*) Yes, I'm going to have twins!

Anyway, I'm adding a new scene that wasn't in the book where Frankie picks up a serviceman in a bar.

PANCHO: (*to Carson*) When I was on shore leave, I met a young girl in a Decatur Street bar who looked like a tomboy – a waif.

18

CARSON: Oh, this is good – the type of experience I want. My Frankie or in Spanish: Panchita – Right, Pancho? – is a tomboy.

TENN: I see our guest is improving her Spanish. I guess that's making her burn the midnight oil. Right, Pancho?

PANCHO: (*interrupting*) My señorita was a boy – and he took it up the ass.

CARSON: Oh, my! Are you listening, Brother-Man?

PANCHO: Brother-Man?

CARSON: It's an endearment of address that we Southerners use for friends and family. Right, Brother-Man?

TENN: I'll toast to that, Sister-Woman!

CARSON: Sorry for interrupting, Pancho.

CARSON returns to her writing.

PANCHO begins to leaf through her manuscript.

PANCHO: (*to Tenn*) She's dedicating *Member of the Wedding* to her loving husband. The one she's invited for a three-way with me.

TENN: Now, Pancho, that isn't mineral water you're guzzling. Don't go having one of your conniptions again.

PANCHO ignores him and continues drinking. He turns his focus to TENN's manuscript.

PANCHO: (*enraged*) Why isn't he dedicating *Summer and Smoke* to me – instead of Sister-Woman?

TENN: I will not tolerate such outbursts when I am working.

PANCHO: Shut up. It's all lies. Tenn, you say you love me? Carson, you say you're my friend?

CARSON: Of course, we are dear friends. I've spoken highly about you to Reeves, and he's dying to meet you.

TENN and CARSON continue their typing like twin pianists at either end of the table.

PANCHO retreats to the sofa, and finds his guitar.

He plays "La Golondrina." His passionate rendition at times rises above the cacophonous typing from the other artists who occasionally burst into arias from their writing.

TENN removes a manuscript page from his typewriter as a journalist might tear a headline from a teletype machine.

TENN: (*reading*) "I feel like a water lily on a Chinese lagoon. Won't you sit down? My name is Alma. Spanish for soul! What's yours?"

TENN returns to his work. CARSON repeats the same action.

CARSON: (*reading*) "The trouble with me is that for a long time, I have been just an 'I' person. All other people can say 'we.' All people belong to a 'we' except me. Not belonging to a 'we' makes you too lonesome."

CARSON returns to her work.

TENN: (*reading, while focusing on Pancho*) "The only angel in Glorious Hill is that one. And its heart is made of granite and its blood runs mineral water."

TENN returns to his work.

When PANCHO finishes, he pauses expecting the others to break into applause. No such luck.

Finally in desperation, or in a newfound realization, he moves to the door.

PANCHO: (*locking the door*) Now, who wants to be first?

He starts to undress.

The typing stops.

BLACKOUT.

༄༅

SCENE FIVE

HOLLYWOOD TO NEW ORLEANS. FALL 1946.

The stage is dark – spot on PANCHO.

As he speaks, he is cleaning the mess left from the previous scene.

PANCHO: In September, Tenn and I went West to Hollywood as house guests of Tenn's producer, Irene Mayer Selznick, wife of David O. Selznick.

Tenn was there to cast the role of the sister who comes to visit in "Poker Night" – and he did.

The actresses up for the leading role were unbelievable: Bette Davis, Margaret Sullivan, Joan Crawford.

My choice: a toss-up between Davis who proved herself with a Latin lover in *Bordertown* and Crawford who of course was born in San Antonio.

As for me, I was in heaven. I had only read about these people in movie magazines I bought at the Eagle Pass drugstore or watched in movies or newsreels at the Joy Rio Theater.

And just like that I was staying in their mansions.

We arrived on the Southwest Chief and were immediately driven to the Beverly Hills estate of the famous movie director George Cukor for a reception.

There were a lot of male starlets at his parties – most were young *maricones* – you know the type – who drift around like matches in the gutter and eventually go down the sewer.

Mister Cukor said I could be an actor. He liked my profile and Latin looks. I reminded him of Ramon Novarro.

21

No, thanks, I told him. Besides, I don't think I can act, but I really liked being around beautiful people.

I swam every day. At first I resembled a pale, floating water lily in Irene's pool. But when she let me borrow her red coupe and drive to the Santa Monica beach, I could lay in the sand and work on a tan.

Now I am brown as an Indio and have nice visible muscles everywhere. Know what I mean?

He gropes himself.

Of course, I behaved myself – doing everything I could for Tenn's comfort and ease, hoping that he'd include me in all the parties and get-togethers.

Still I wasn't invited when Tenn met with Greta Garbo.

My circumstances? I'm a parasite to Tennessee. With living expenses as high as they are, a weekly allowance is all I get from him, but I am happy.

It isn't that I erase my mind from my obligations. It's that I love Tenn, and I feel some gap when I'm not near him. He has done much for me, and if I am patient, and prove myself worthy, I will not regret it later.

California is a good place to live, but unless you have a very good job, you will be unhappy.

There are thousands of Mexicans in LA, and they are typical of the people back in San Antonio. And in Los Angeles – "Los An-gel-es," the same prejudices exist – poor paying jobs, lack of respect.

I experienced this first hand at a John Huston soirée for Tenn. I was mistaken for a waiter even though I was wearing my Brooks Brothers tux! Instead of refilling some gringo's drink, I threw it in his face.

I was driving home after a delicious Mexican meal at Olvera Plaza when I spotted a hitchhiker at the corner of Santa Monica and La Brea. With his cowlick hair and cowboy jeans, he looked like he had just come off a Texas ranch.

Now, you've listened to *Twenty Questions* on the radio. Can you figure out who he was? Okay, one clue, he was the most decorated American soldier in World War II.

Yep, it was Audie Murphy. How could I not recognize him? He said he came out to get into acting after receiving an invitation and passage from the actor James Cagney.

When I asked about Cagney, Audie just shrugged. He said he was now living at the YMCA on La Cienega. I wanted to invite him to meet the Selznicks but thought better. Irene later said that Cagney hired him as a gardener and allowed him to live in his servant's quarters.

If that was the way they treated a national hero in Hollywood, I never wanted to return. And somehow my own military snafu didn't seem so *fatale*.

Both Tenn and I were eager to get back to work in New Orleans, the "City that Care Forgot." Tenn to his writing and me to my sales job at the Maison Blanche department store on Canal.

On our return trip, Tenn insisted I stop in Texas to visit my family. I hadn't been home since my discharge from the service. I was reluctant at first – the black sheep returning and all that – but it did me good – because now I know why I left in the first place, and why I never want to go back.

PANCHO puts away his broom and dust pan and retrieves a suit of clothes.

He changes into his evening clothes.

We're in New Orleans again.

Believe me, New Orleans is the most tolerant city in America and with trade from South America increasing, it is the number one city for us Latin Americans.

Tenn's grandfather, the Rev. Walter Dakin arrived this morning, and I was deeply impressed. The old gentleman is remarkable and even has a gay twinkle in his eye. He'll stay with us until next week when we motor to Florida for a few days.

Right now, Mister Dakin is resting, Tennessee is inside working on a short story, *y su humilde servidor* is getting ready to go out to Lafitte's for a nightcap.

BLACKOUT.

୫୨୦୧ଓ

SCENE SIX

NEW ORLEANS. TENN & PANCHO'S APARTMENT. HOURS LATER.

PANCHO enters after a night of carousing.

Since TENN's light is still on, PANCHO slowly takes off his shoes and tip-toes into the room.

He trips over a door stop – putting an index finger to his lips in a gesture of "quiet please."

PANCHO takes off his shirt, carefully placing it on a hanger. He then surveys the room, as if searching for some sign of betrayal.

He stands over TENN who has fallen asleep while toiling at his typewriter.

PANCHO picks up a manuscript folder and begins to read quietly.

PANCHO: (*reading*) "Rubio y Morena," a short story by Tennessee Williams.

"The writer had many acquaintances, especially now that his name had begun to acquire some public luster. And he also had a few friends which he had kept over the years the way that you keep a few books you have read several times but are unwilling to part with.

"In order to make more understandable the relationship with which the story deals, a rather singular relationship between the writer and the Mexican girl AMADA began in the Mexican border town of Laredo, one summer during the war when he was returning from a trip through the Mexican interior."

TENN: (*startled*) Pancho! What are you doing creeping around like that?

PANCHO: Ah, I caught you writing masturbation fantasies again.

And what is this stuff about AMADA? My name is AMADO. Amado Francisco Rodriguez y Gonzalez.

If anyone is a puta, it's you.

He says this softly, playfully.

A decorated Mexican funeral wreath dangles nearby and catches his attention.

PANCHO: Estúpido, don't you have any respect? These wreaths aren't Mardi Gras decorations. They're funeral wreaths to place on the graves of dead – los muertos.

Where did you get this one? Is it new? Mother made and sold tin flower wreaths in the market – they last a lifetime.

TENN: *Flores por los muertos?*

PANCHO: No, querido. It's *para* not *por. Para* means 'for' and *por* means 'by.' But your Spanish is improving.

TENN: Gracias. Oh, Amado, I was wondering if your brother Juancho got that sales job at Godchaux's?

PANCHO: What do you mean "got the job"? You made a pass at him?

TENN: No, chico. I wrote a letter of recommendation to my – our friend – the manager of men's furnishings.

PANCHO: You don't remember trying to grope my little brother?

TENN: Little? I dare say that's not how I would describe him.

PANCHO: (*angrily*) *No me importa una chingada* if you sleep with an entire fleet, but you do not touch my brother. He's off-limits.

TENN: Off limits? Then why are all those off-limits bars filled with straight sailors? Can't you see, it's healthy for a young man to experiment.

PANCHO: If you must know, one of those young sailors came here the other night while you were in Dallas with Margo. He was tall, blond and hung like a stallion.

TENN: Are we keeping secrets, dear heart?

PANCHO: It was your brother – Dakin. He was on leave and wanted to stay here. So I let him. And if anyone has raging hormones, it's he.

TENN: So now the iguana slithers from under its rock. Touche.

I watched over my baby brother when we were children, and I still feel responsible for him.

PANCHO: And I, my brother's keeper.

When I came in last night I heard this racket coming from the bath where you seem to lock yourself away.

Were you beating off or getting served?

TENN: I beg your pardon. It's you who is always bringing strangers into our home.

PANCHO: That's a laugh.

I have always depended on strangers – strangers like you.

TENN: That never bothered you before. Next you'll be hiring a private dick to watch my every move.

PANCHO: And now you are writing my family into your stories. You lying son of a bitch.

I told you those stories in confidence – not to broadcast them in public.

TENN: Perdón. I don't think I was ever trying to do any such thing. I was only learning from your background – to enrich my own paltry one. And like it or not Pancho Rodriguez, you are part of my life, my Mexican muse. You inspire me.

Isn't inspiration the most precious act of love one can give another?

Just don't try reading between the lines like our brothers or Margo are trying to do.

PANCHO: Well, I'm going to put an end to this now.

TENN: Oh, Pancho. Don't!

TENN rises to keep PANCHO from throwing his manuscript out of the window. They struggle.

PANCHO: Ladrón. This is all lies. I've been waiting for this moment a long time.

TENN: I promise to keep you out of the damn story. It's about two sisters – not two brothers.

PANCHO: You turned us into drag queens?

TENN: No, no, that's not it. It's my experiences.

PANCHO picks up the manuscript, tears it into pieces that scatter on the floor.

PANCHO: Bombs Away! It's over. Fin. The end.

PANCHO storms out of the room.

The sound of breaking dishes punctuates his movement as he makes his way downstairs.

Then a moment of silence in the room.

TENN contemplates what it's like to be without PANCHO.

PANCHO: (*shouts from the street*) Tenn! Tenn! Come out here, cabrón.

A pause and then a long violent wail:

CAAABROOON!

The sound of PANCHO's voice hangs in the air.

TENN in desperation rushes out toward a clinging reconciliation on the street below.

TENN: (*O.S.*) Yes, baby.

BLACKOUT.

END OF ACT ONE

Act Two

SCENE ONE

PROVINCETOWN. RANCHO PANCHO. SUMMER 1947.

> *PANCHO enters with a paint brush. He has paint spots on his clothing and his body.*

PANCHO: Yuck! Rancho Pancho. What a dump.

> Provincetown is gloomier than Nantucket was last year.

> It's good we're touching up the outside: red, white and green. The colors of the Mexican flag – now it looks like a real Texas rancho. Our guests Margo and Joanna can feel right at home.

TENN: It isn't called Rancho Pancho for nothing.

PANCHO: (*as Rita Hayworth*) "If I'd been a ranch, they would've named me the Bar Nothing."

> *PANCHO waits patiently for TENN to respond to his movie quote.*

TENN: (*contemplating*) The line comes from a Western. Oh, I know.

> *My Darling Clementine.* John Ford. Linda Darnell. 1946.

PANCHO: *Gilda.* 1946. Rita Hayworth.

TENN: Try me again. Make it easier. I mentioned your favorite Linda Darnell. Shouldn't I get a point for that?

PANCHO: Agreed. This one is like pitching soft ball.

"I'm trash, trash, trash."

TENN: You're trying to trick me. That's *Gilda* again.

PANCHO: *Duel in the Sun.* 1946. King Vidor. Jennifer Jones.

TENN: Princess. We never saw that film. Not fair.

PANCHO: Not you, but me, at the Loew's State on Canal. You were in New York that weekend with Margo. Remember?

But we're in luck, it's showing this weekend here in P-Town.

I love the film. Jennifer Jones is Pearl Chavez, who is so like me – Mexican, brown as an Indio, born in a Texas border town – and in love with a gringo two-timer.

In another life, I'd want to return as Pearl and avenge my lover's betrayal.

TENN: I didn't think Jennifer Jones had that kind of talent.

Irene never mentioned her for "Poker Night."

PANCHO: She has talent in spades. Her acting range is far-reaching – from her Oscar-winning role as Bernadette of Lourdes (*he cross himself*) to a best actress nomination for Pearl Chavez (*he puts his hands on his hips*) – from saint to sinner – in two years. Like me.

And it's a Selznick Studio production. Are you game?

TENN: Let's. However, for Jennifer to remind me of you, she'd have to go from saint to sinner in two hours flat.

PANCHO: Irene never mentioned her for the role because Miss Jones is shacking up with Mister Selznick. And once his divorce from Irene is final, I bet they'll tie the knot.

TENN: Oh, Princess, I never discuss personal matters with my producer; neither does she.

PANCHO: Why do you keep calling me Princess?

TENN: Because her royal highness, Miss Queen is alive and thriving – although presently in exile like the Pirate Lafitte.

Besides, Princess was your sobriquet when we recorded those skits at the Pennyland Arcade.

A command performance, milady?

TENN removes the cover from the sofa which PANCHO transforms into a cape, a lamp shade crown completes his drag as the fey PRINCESS RODRIGUEZ.

TENN: (*as reporter*) This is Vanilla Williams, your roving reporter on the street. And I am speaking to the Princess Rodriguez.

Hello, Princess. How did you find N'Awlins?

PANCHO: (*with thick Latin accent*) Oh, vunderful. I took a tour of Decatur Street.

TENN: The Decadence Tour is what they call it. All those young sailors from Greece, Italy, the Encantadas.

PANCHO: Yes. And I even took the trolley on Canal to Magazine and T-Chopa-tou-las.

TENN: Why I do declare, Princess. No decent royalty should be found on those streets. Decatur is fine, by day, but never by night.

You never know who's going to bump into you. If you get my drift.

PANCHO: Oh, I thought that was the point.

They burst out laughing, hugging and kissing in their joy.

PANCHO: Are those recordings around here?

TENN: They better not be. We'll be ruined.

> I wired my agent Madame Wood the opening scene for a new play set in Acapulco.

> "Quebrada" – where bronze divers comb the deep blue sea for iridescent pearls to bestow on their beloved.

PANCHO: (*singing a refrain*) "Acuérdate de Acapulco, de aquellas noches, María bonita, María del alma."

> That's the only Acapulco I know – a Mexican lullaby my mother taught me when I was a child.

> You however have travelled through the interior of Mexico, seen the pyramids, lived in la capital.

> All I've known is the god-damn border and María Bonita.

> Perhaps after "Poker Night"?

TENN: (*singing*) "South of the border, down Mexico way."

PANCHO: Can we really make that trip? You may be stuck in New York for months if it's a hit.

TENN: Don't worry your handsome face about it, wrinkles are unbecoming at any age.

PANCHO: (*looking in the mirror*) Are you expecting your agent or your director?

TENN: Neither. An actor Marlon Brando is arriving by bus to audition.

> Oh, before that, we got to wash up and get the bedroom ready for Margo and Joanna. They'll be here tonight.

PANCHO: But I thought John Garfield had the part?

TENN: Too much like you, baby. A prima donna.

PANCHO: Isn't that Stanley character the one we recorded at the arcade on Royal?

TENN: (*mocking*) Royal? You used to say *Camino Real*. Are you losing your Spanish or are you patronizing me?

PANCHO: Well, if you sleep with gringos, you wake up with...

TENN: ...*abajo con los gringos*!

PANCHO: Well, señor, you're in a reactionary mood.

TENN: You've forgotten opposites attract. What is that Spanish expression...*like dirt*....

PANCHO: *Como mugre y uña*. As close as dirt under a fingernail. And that's damn closer than we've been in quite a while.

TENN: Tu y yo?

PANCHO: Now, after you finish this cattle call as Mister Cukor says.

TENN: Cukor? When did he say something to you? Did you, did he?

PANCHO: That maricón? Heavens, no.

> Besides, he wasn't interested in me. He rather fancied you, but you were so busy being Miss Queen Bee that he soon tired of the pursuit.

> He-he-he-he-he, the Shadow knows.

> My spies tell me, he's known as Doctor Sugar, the cruelest old bitch in Hollywoodland.

> Cukorwicz or Cukor = sugar or some such Polish variation.

TENN: Why hadn't you told me any of this before!

PANCHO: Stop! I know where you're going with this. Don't turn it into another reason to dump me.

> I've read those letters that you carelessly leave around, complaining about your "Mexican Problem" to Margo and the rest of the Weird Sisters.

> Now that this Marley Brandy is coming over –

TENN : – It's Marlon Brando. And no, I'm not interested, besides I hear he's straighter than –

PANCHO: – Me? Isn't that what you're getting at?

They move to the kitchen.

TENN runs tap water to fill a glass.

TENN: Princess, this audition means a lot. Let's stop bickering. After the "cattle call," we'll go into town and get drunk. I want you – us to be happy.

PANCHO: What happened to the water?

TENN: What!

PANCHO: There's no running water.

TENN turns the faucet off and on, but no water issues.

PANCHO tries the kitchen light switch.

PANCHO: Ni electricidad!

Did you pay the deposit for the utilities?

TENN: I certainly did. Perhaps a water main burst or a power line is down.

PANCHO: Or some rodent lodged itself in the pipes or fried itself chewing on the wires.

TENN: Do something! Call a repairman. Something. Our guests are arriving tout de suite.

God, I wish there was a man around the house!

PANCHO grabs TENN by the collar and pushes him against the wall.

PANCHO: Just stop. I'm getting very pissed, maricón.

TENN: Just unhand me.

PANCHO: Not until you promise – swear – there isn't any other man in your life. No one. Just me. That's all I need. Your word.

PANCHO unhands TENN. He looks at TENN as if a stranger.

TENN: I've always treated you with the kindness I reserve for my dearest and most cherished – my family.

As your madrecita said when we met: Comprende, estúpido?

PANCHO: I apologize. I'm wrong. Without you, I'm nothing. Nada.

When I was at home or in the service, they provided everything. Then I met you. I was certain you were the one.

Para siempre, forever.

TENN: Para siempre is a damn long time, chico. I get older and you get younger. We've fooled ourselves for nearly two years. How much longer –

PANCHO: – Fooled? Fooled who? Certainly not me.

I know what's been going on in New Orleans, the men you lure to our place on St. Peter's and your string of one-night stands.

You're right. I'm the one who still doesn't get it. Perhaps I need to move on.

TENN: And yet you are the best thing in my life since...

PANCHO: Go ahead. Only consenting adults are present.

TENN: ...since Kip and a few others.

PANCHO: The young man you were cruising as I was getting our baggage?

TENN: No. Kip dumped me. Afterward, I was dead. That's when I went to Mexico.

You saved my life just like that time I was dying in Taos. The doctors in St. Louis has said there was nothing wrong with my health, but once in New Mexico, that nothing turned into diverticulitis.

PANCHO: The nurses wouldn't let me see you. I wasn't the next of kin.

I still have scars from scaling the second story ledge trying to get into your hospital bed. And I'd do it again.

If risking life and limb isn't love then, as the song says, "it will have to do..."

TENN: "... until the real thing comes along."

PANCHO: And the sailor?

TENN: Frank? He was pleased that I had such a handsome companion.

He isn't as inelegant as you. He's quiet, gentle and –

PANCHO: Hung! I saw him "quietly and gently" groping himself.

No, you're right. NO PASSION there. Just slam-bang, thank you, Memphis, Tennessee and Macon, Georgia.

TENN: You don't leave a person anything, do you?

PANCHO: No dowry, sorry. I'm a poor Mexican.

TENN: You carry your race as if it were a brown badge of courage.

PANCHO: I don't need any stinking badges.

TENN: And I'm a man with desires. And yes, there have been others, but you haven't the right to shame me.

PANCHO: A few others? Twenty? Thirty? Am I getting warm? Forty? I'm getting tired. Sixty?

TENN throws his drink at PANCHO's face.

They grapple violently until it becomes a primal embrace.

Half-undressed, they lunge toward the sofa.

PANCHO: What about the water and power? You have an audition.

TENN: (*his hand over Pancho's mouth*) Fuck the plumbing. Screw the audition.

BLACKOUT.

∞ ☙

SCENE TWO

RANCHO PANCHO. LATER THAT AFTERNOON.

> *TENN and PANCHO sit on the sofa in the afterglow of lovemaking. Half-dressed, they share a cigarette and a drink.*

TENN: That actor is hours late. You don't suppose he got lost?

PANCHO: Want me to go to the bars and cast a net for him? I am a pretty good fisherman.

TENN: I guess a line from Crane or Wilde would be appropriate, but I'll take the director's word on this one. He swears this young man is Stanley Kowalski.

PANCHO: Kowalski? I thought he was going to be Latin – not Czech.

TENN: Polish.

PANCHO: You can't be serious. How many Polacks do you see in New Orleans? He should be Latin American – like you originally planned.

TENN: Now, Pancho you must realize Dame Selznick is trying to reach a wider cross section of the audience.

PANCHO: What? That's an oxymoron. Polacks don't go to the theater.

And, as far as I know, there isn't a law against the mating of Mexicans and Anglos. Or is there?

TENN: Bravo. Where in heaven's name, did you ever pick up a word like oxymoron?

PANCHO: Just something Doctor Sugar said about an actress. I had to look it up. Then I put it in my diary.

TENN: Why you sly, young devil.

Well, I don't know any Latins who might bring that animal magnetism required of the part. Do you?

After a pause.

PANCHO: Yes. Anthony Quinn is perfect.

I'd like to pride myself in thinking that maybe this character has a little bit of me in him.

After all, I played the part on those recordings.

TENN: *Abajo con los gringos*!

TENN lifts a drink in mock homage.

PANCHO: Quinn has a bigger name in Hollywood than twenty Brandys. He's even married to Katherine DeMille.

TENN: Oh, yes. Cecil B. DeMille's daughter – big frigging deal.

You must realize that a theater actor is much different than a Hollywood star.

PANCHO: I'd rather be a Hollywood actor than a stage unknown. Irene told me I had the makings of an actor. And a handsome one at that.

TENN: And I couldn't agree more.

TENN lures PANCHO to the sofa. He has more lovemaking on his mind.

Loud knock at the front door. Before either can move, the door opens.

Enter MARGO.

PANCHO and especially TENN are taken aback.

PANCHO: Margo? You're early.

TENN still in a daze over Margo's intrusion remains silent – leaving MARGO and PANCHO to duke it out.

MARGO: (*reacting to the paint on Pancho*) You've finally done it, Pancho. Given Texas back to the Mexicans.

PANCHO: I figured you'd be you're usual charming self, so I put my war paint on, Colonel Custer!

MARGO: I may have the last laugh. I hear you're about to be evicted from Rancho Pancho by its Southern landlord.

And I'm not whistling Dixie.

Now help us unload, it was a long drive. Joanna is out in the car, she isn't feeling well.

Where's the ladies room?

PANCHO: The plumbing and the electricity are on the blink. We're still waiting for a repairman.

You'll have to do your business in the dunes. Just like a real Texas pioneer woman.

MARGO: (*to Joanna*) The toilet is out. We'll have to go in the dunes.

MARGO exits. Blowing a kiss at TENN. PANCHO waits until they leave then shouts out after them.

PANCHO: Super Cunts versus Sand Crabs.

PANCHO returns to the sofa and TENN's arms.

MARGO: (*O.S.*) Don't you have any toilet paper?

Frustrated, PANCHO goes to the door.

PANCHO: Use leaves.

MARGO: (*O.S.*) There aren't any – just sand.

PANCHO: Use Kotex!

> (*to Tenn*) Or better yet – a pine cone.

> I better go out there and bring in their luggage; otherwise, we'll never hear the end of this.

> *PANCHO exits.*

> *Loud knock at the back door.*

TENN: It's about time. This guy better know something about plumbing. I hope neither of the girls is on the rag. Otherwise, Whowee.

> *TENN opens the kitchen door.*

TENN: You arrived in a nick of time, young man.

> *BRANDO stands off-stage. His voice can be heard but his person cannot be seen.*

BRANDO: (*O.S.*) I apologize for being late, but I took the wrong Port Authority bus. It stopped in every frigging burg along the way.

TENN: Do you know anything about plumbing and electricity?

> We have guests and we're all having to shit outside and grope our way in the dark.

BRANDO: (*O.S.*) An actor has to be a Jack of all trades, sir.

> You never know when you might have to clean a clogged toilet or mop up an overflowing sink.

> Hand me that wrench, and I'll clear the pipes underneath the house. I'll have your privy flushing better than the Meadows in no time.

As for the lights, a Lincoln penny in the fuse box works every time.

BRANDO exits.

TENN: Finally, a real man in fairyland.

PANCHO enters with the luggage.

TENN: He's fixing the lights and clearing the plumbing.

My kingdom for a butch handyman!

TENN moves to the living room as MARGO rushes in.

MARGO: Tenn! Tenn! Brando is outside – working on the plumbing.

TENN and MARGO rush out – off-stage.

PANCHO is left holding the bags.

The lights come on throughout the house, the water is flowing in the sink and music is heard from the radio.

PANCHO turns off the kitchen faucets and then the radio.

He stands alone in the silent Rancho – a forgotten man.

Outside, he hears laughter, a hush, and then Brando reading.

BRANDO: (*O.S.*) "Listen, baby, when we first met – you and me – you thought I was common. Well, how right you was. I was common as dirt.

"And wasn't we happy together? Wasn't it all OK? Till she showed here. Hoity-toity, describing me like a ape."

MARGO: (*O.S.*) Oh Tenn. Your writing is pure genius.

TENN: (*O.S.*) As they say, Margo, write what you know about.

MARGO: (*O.S.*) Absolutely. And I knew all along Brando was perfect for this part.

41

PANCHO is devastated – Stanley's words hit home.

TENN: (*O.S.*) Now, are we out to the bars to celebrate, or is this some kind of Joycean wake for the dead?

Off-stage, TENN breaks out in drunken chorus.

"Down in the Valley, valley so deep. I met a young lover who I would not keep."

PANCHO turns out the lights and joins them off-stage.

BLACKOUT.

∞∞

SCENE THREE

LATER, RANCHO PANCHO.

A drunken PANCHO enters.

PANCHO: Where? Am I dead? Tenn in the car? Is he hurt?

Hello. Anybody home? Where are you, lying son-of-a-bitch?

TENN is asleep on the sofa.

PANCHO: Get up, you miserable excuse of a lover.

TENN: (*startled*) Pancho?

Get out. God-damn it, you almost killed me, ass-hole.

PANCHO: (*ignoring Tenn*) Where is the cocksucker you took off with?

TENN: Pancho, I wanted to celebrate, and I had a little to drink, and Frank suggested we go somewhere quiet and talk. Nada mas.

PANCHO: We just screwed on this sofa this afternoon. Didn't that mean anything?

Now that you got that stupid Brandy cast, I thought we'd have more time together. Just us.

42

TENN: You don't remember what you did, do you? Well, tell it to the Army maybe they'll believe you – this time.

TENN stands, facing PANCHO. He appears a young boy caught red-handed playing with matches.

After I gave Frank a ride home, I went back to the Atlantic House bar. You were no place to be found.

Brando and his girlfriend left early as did Margo and Joanna. I figured you were here at the Rancho too.

But my car was gone. I started to walk back and got as far as the top of the hill when I saw the headlights of a car careening wildly toward me.

If the fog hadn't been heavy near the marsh, you would have killed me. I know it was you – yelling and cursing in Spanish.

With me dead, what the hell will you have? Nada. What would you have proven? Nada. You'd have ended up on death row, then what?

PANCHO: (*apologetic*) I didn't mean –

TENN: Shush.

"Sometimes I know exactly what you're going to say. Most of the time. The other times … the other times, you're just a stinker."

To Have and Have Not. 1944. Howard Hawks. Lauren Bacall and BOGIE!

PANCHO – twixt laughing and crying – falls to his knees.

TENN stands over him – his repentant lover finally at his feet.

But dear Pancho, I am here – alive. And I love you the same as I did this afternoon.

PANCHO: I'm sick and tired of your 'dear boy, this,' and 'my dear boy, that.'

You swear you love me, and the first chance you get, you're out humping some Popeye.

You used to want to pleasure me, now the only person you satisfy is yourself.

TENN: We'll go to Mexico after the opening, I promise.

I'm under a lot of pressure. You don't help matters by not giving me room to move around. It's suffocating being around you.

I can't have any new friends or see old ones, because you think I'm cheating.

You've become so insecure, you're probably jealous of your own shadow.

PANCHO: Insecure? What about you – writing about people you know nothing about. You imitate the best and the rest you get your friends or strangers to supply details and dialogue.

You thought you were so daring taking me to Dallas for Margo's show and then parading me in front of those Baptist bigots.

Never once did you ask me how I felt being shamed like some exotic savage on exhibit.

Maybe you should have shackled me in chains or put me on a leash just in case I growled too loud or spoke out of turn.

PANCHO moves to the kitchen to get a drink.

TENN: Oh, Pancho, bring me one too?

PANCHO: There, see what I mean: It's 'Pancho, get me this, or 'Pancho, do that'.

I risked everything I knew and had by leaving Texas with a perfect stranger!

My family believes I've abandoned and betrayed them by choosing you.

Women would give anything for a man like me. No strings attached. But you won't catch me kissing and telling, about my conquests or sneaking off behind your back.

And you never listen to me. All you do is write everything down. That's not love.

And, to make it worse, you take all of this, and instead of turning it into magic, you turn the Gonzales' into a brown face minstrel show for your *Summer and Smoke* mierda.

Shaming me and insulting my family name.

Reading your stuff, one would think the Old South won the war.

Wake up, cabrón, they lost.

PANCHO sits on the sofa, exhausted.

TENN is stunned by Pancho's rage, and hurt by his brutal attack on his work.

TENN: (*trying to regain his composure*) After I left the bar, I wanted to come back and hang the portrait I had made especially for your birthday. It arrived yesterday.

I had a duplicate sent to your mother and father in Texas. So they could be as delighted as I am about how dashing and handsome you've become.

TENN starts to unwrap the painting.

PANCHO Did that old bitch – the artist – mention I posed in my best Brooks Brother suit? But it was the wrong look. I didn't look Latin enough!

Then she demanded I take off my coat, then the tie, my pants, and finally – I had to bare my cojones.

He begins to undress.

TENN: Oh, a strip tease. That's the spirit.

45

Bring a bottle, and I'll turn the radio on – only we better not wake up the girls.

PANCHO: Get it yourself, you pinche maricón.

TENN: Pancho, don't tease – just STRIP.

PANCHO: I've got a surprise for you too.

PANCHO strips down to his briefs, edging TENN toward him.

TENN: This is so naughty. I'm down on my hands and knees. Come to Mama.

PANCHO picks up a kitchen knife and holds it to TENN's neck.

PANCHO: Now, show me exactly how you went down on that fucking sailor.

TENN: (*sobbing*) No, please, don't. I'll never do it again.

TENN and PANCHO struggle as the knife falls to the floor. They exchange blows. Seizing the moment, TENN runs out into the night.

PANCHO stands frozen, the knife once again clenched in his hand.

Lights inside flicker as a mistral slams the open door.

PANCHO takes the knife to the wrapped painting.

It is a portrait of a young Mexican peon dressed in white linen: a symbolic rendering of all he left in another life.

He approaches the painting and stabs it over and over.

He collapses to his knees, a defeated Indian brave.

PANCHO: The prodigal son is dead. *Qué Viva El PUTO!!*

BLACKOUT

ಬಂಛ

SCENE FOUR

RANCHO PANCHO. MADRUGADA.

A bedraggled TENN enters. He stops before a figure covered by a blanket on the sofa.

TENN: (*softly*) Oh, Pancho. Are you feeling better, sweetie?

I am so sorry that I let you down. But you know how it is with me, a few drinks and I'm putty in any man's arms.

No response from the sofa.

No, that's not true. I was thinking of you the entire time. How can I make it up?

Let's skip New York and drive on to New Haven. Rehearsals won't start for days. We can be alone. Just us.

Please don't hate me, *mi querido amante, te amo.*

No response not even snoring.

Are you dead?

The figure on the sofa turns over. It is MARGO.

MARGO: Too late. He didn't even pack a bag. Who knows where he was headed – Texas, Mexico, maybe New Orleans if he hasn't burned his bridges there too.

MARGO sits up and lights a cigarette.

MARGO: I gave him the money you put aside. Two weeks advance. And fare for his bus ticket.

TENN: Let's go to the bus depot. I never meant for you to give him that money. It was just to put him on notice that I wouldn't put up with his nonsense any longer.

I never meant to send him away. He is all I have, sweetheart.

MARGO: Joanna took him to the station. He was in worse shape than you.

TENN: Then he needs medical attention. I could never forgive myself if something happened to him because of an indiscretion on my part.

Where are my car keys? I'll drive if you won't help.

MARGO: They're in the car – out on the dunes.

But you won't be going anywhere with four blown tires and a busted radiator.

The fool tried to run you over and all you can say is that he needs a doctor.

TENN: But I want Pancho back.

MARGO: Now, now. When we heard the commotion, I called the police.

They're out searching for you.

TENN: When he came at me, I just ran and ran. I must have fallen in the sand and cried myself to sleep.

MARGO: It's nearly dawn. You need your sleep. Joanna and I are leaving.

Just remember who your real friends are. I also hope you can get me and Joanna a job on this "Poker Game" project.

TENN: But we already have a director.

MARGO: You said that I did such a great job on "Smoke" that I had the better chance – nobody knows your work better than me!

TENN: It's all in Irene's hands. I had nothing to do with it. You have my word.

MARGO: Pancho was right. He said you told everyone I did a terrible job of directing, and you made no qualms about broadcasting that to Missy Selznick.

He calls us the Weird Sisters – like those hags in the "Scottish play." I never knew he could read – much less Shakespeare.

TENN: Don't talk about Pancho. It's bad enough I made him get –

TENN falters. He navigates to the sofa.

MARGO: Do you want to lie down?

(*touching his forehead*) You've got a fever. Shouldn't I call a doctor?

TENN: I'll be fine. I just need rest. I'll sleep on the sofa in case Pancho returns.

MARGO: Well, suit yourself. You might be right. That type always returns to the scene of the crime.

Want me to turn out the lights?

TENN: Leave the curtains open. The blue lights of the stars soothe the savage beast.

MARGO: By the way, we found this weird monstrosity in the bedroom closet as we were hanging our clothes. It fell, and the sharp tin cut Joanna's finger.

Is it a Mardi Gras decoration? Shouldn't you put it in a safer place?

MARGO holds the Mexican funeral wreath and hands it to TENN who gently takes the wreath, and cleaves unto it, as if to a newborn babe.

TENN: "It's the stuff dreams are made of, Kiddo!"

The Maltese Falcon. John Huston. Humphrey Bogart and …

MARGO: Mary Astor, 1941.

MARGO kisses TENN and exits.

A somnambulant TENN then rises and straightens the disheveled sofa where he and Pancho made love.

He breathes in the aroma of the spent serape blanket, unfolding it to tuck in a weary sleeper – or to cover a corpse.

TENN places the tattered portrait of Pancho and the Mexican wreath on the sofa as one might decorate a funeral bier or a Day of the Dead altar.

He moves to his writing desk, sits, as a pianist might in front of a baby grand piano.

TENN concentrates on the blue stars, closes his eyes, and begins to type.

A spot on the sofa glows.

Fade to black.

END OF ACT TWO

THE END

Afterword

The Kindness of Strangers

Pancho Rodriguez and Tennessee Williams, New Orleans, 1946.

After the success of *The Glass Menagerie*, Thomas Lanier Williams, later known as Tennessee, spent time in Mexico in late 1945. "I feel I was born in Mexico in another life," he wrote in a letter from Mexico City. Over the years, other writers — from Katherine Anne Porter to Williams' mentor, Hart Crane — had expressed the same sentiment. But luck was with Williams as he crossed *la frontera* at Piedras Negras/Eagle Pass: He met Pancho Rodriguez, a young Mexican American. The tale of that meeting would later be embellished — with Williams' car breaking down and a border guard's son helping to rescue a manuscript that INS officials had confiscated.

The rising 34-year-old playwright was immediately smitten with the 24-year-old Pancho — the border guard's son — and invited him to New Orleans as his live-in muse. The rest, as they say, is history. But the chronicle of their relationship was forgotten and, to a large extent, whitewashed from Williams' life story.

I met Pancho Rodriguez in the mid-1970s, when I was teaching summer classes at Loyola University in New Orleans. I knew that he had been a close friend of Williams, but Pancho and his brother Johnny were more interested in news of relatives in the Eagle Pass/Crystal City area, where I used to live.

Years later, I was a neophyte playwright with a few credits to my name and a fellowship to write Tejano stories for the theater. While exploring the possibility that the Williams-Rodriguez affair had the stuff for good theater, I came upon *My Life*, Elia Kazan's autobiography. Kazan, who directed both the stage and film versions of *A Streetcar Named Desire*, writes about his difficulty understanding the love-hate relationship between Stanley and Blanche in a play now considered among the best of the twentieth century. But it all became clear when he witnessed an altercation between Williams and Rodriguez: "If Tennessee was Blanche, Pancho was Stanley."

That became my mantra as I traveled to interview those who had known the two during the years they lived together (1945-1947). Most roads led to New Orleans. Coincidentally, their relationship ended when *Streetcar* opened on Broadway. By then Williams had a new muse, Frank Merlo.

At first it seemed I was going nowhere. Regulars at the annual Tennessee Williams Festival in New Orleans shrugged. Some asked if I was confusing Pancho with Merlo. Others felt there was nothing of import to be gleaned. Finally, through friends at Loyola, I reconnected with Pancho's brother Johnny. At first he declined an interview; he had promised Pancho he would never reveal details of the painful affair. Then he warmed up after I reminded him of our Texas connection. We did two short phone conversations, but Johnny died before we could do a sit-down interview.

I did, however, hear from Virginia Spencer Carr, a biographer of Katherine Anne Porter and Carson McCullers. Carr had interviewed Pancho at length about the summer of 1946, when he and Williams entertained McCullers at their Nantucket bungalow, which Williams had dubbed "Rancho Pancho." Both writers worked together during that summer: McCullers on a stage version of her novel, *The Member of the Wedding*, and Williams on a rewrite of *Summer and Smoke*, which now included a Mexican family in Eagle Pass/Piedras Negras named Gonzalez (Pancho's maternal last name).

Even through poetic language, it was easy to identify the play's inspiration. In its final scene, a traveling salesman asks Miss Alma Winemiller if she speaks Spanish. *Poquito*, she answers, to which he replies, "Sometimes *poquito* is enough."

Searching in other critical and biographical works proved more daunting: Pancho's name wasn't even listed in the index of *Tennessee Williams: Memoirs*. The playwright informed his readers that he couldn't use his former lover's name for fear of legal action. Nevertheless, he managed to tell their story by renaming Pancho as "Santo." Other writers have also referred to "Santo" and to Williams' other sobriquet for Rodriguez: the Princess.

These clues led me to *Tennessee Williams' Letters to Donald Windham: 1940-1965*. I then received e-mail from Williams collector Joe De Salvo of Faulkner House, the famed bookstore in Pirate's Alley in New Orleans. Johnny left all the materials from Pancho's estate to a nephew. For the most part, the family had been in the dark about Rodriguez's relationship with Williams; the nephew showed little interest. But a sister, whom neither Pancho nor Johnny had ever mentioned, then called. "I have the letters, photos, and other items that might interest you," she said, tantalizing me.

The pieces of the puzzle were beginning to come together. A friend of Windham's informed me that Williams and Pancho had made several cheap, personal recordings at the Pennyland Arcade on Royal Street back in the 1940s — and that they were now part of the New York Public Library theater collection. One featured Williams as reporter Vanilla Williams interviewing the visiting Princess Rodriguez (Pancho) of Monterrey on Decatur Street. "Oh Princess, don't cruise there," Vanilla warns.

"But I thought that was where the action was," the Princess retorts.

Other discs feature Pancho singing in Spanish and Williams reciting poetry. However, the pièce de résistance is a scene from *Streetcar* (nearly two years before its Broadway opening) in which Pancho plays Stanley to Williams' Blanche. My mantra suddenly took new life.

Both Windham and Williams' biographer Lyle Leverich claimed that *Streetcar's* most famous line, "I have always depended on the kindness of strangers," originated with Pancho. According to Johnny Rodriguez, the Mexican street vendor in *Streetcar*, who hawks *"flores para los muertos,"* was based on their mother.

Others, including Gore Vidal, recall that Williams would use Rodriguez to create situations that he would later incorporate into his plays and short stories.

Johnny's estate contained a treasure trove of materials: photographs of Williams and Pancho as young men and as middle-aged gentlemen; letters from Pancho to Johnny, written during trips with Williams to Hollywood and New York; and correspondence from *Streetcar* producer Irene Mayer Selznick, literary agent Audrey Wood, and from Williams himself. The diaries of their trip to Rancho Pancho and of their final visit shortly before Williams' death proved invaluable.

Recently, I found two other Rodriguez sisters willing to speak about their brother, who had remained a muse for Williams until the very end.

During one of their last visits, Williams informed Pancho that he had selected Anthony Quinn and Katy Jurado to star in *The Red Devil Battery Sign*, set on the Texas border in Eagle Pass. Apparently, the news had moved Pancho to tears. Decades earlier, he had argued that the lead character of Stanley in *Streetcar* should have been Mexican American and not Polish, since there were more Latinos than Poles in New Orleans. Moreover, he pointed to the wrought-iron balconies and grand courtyards as a legacy of forty years of Spanish rule. (Scholars say Williams named the character after a friend in St. Louis.) Pancho further argued that the part should go to a Latino because Marlon Brando was unknown. The particular Latino he had in mind: Mexican American actor Anthony Quinn (who, indeed, was cast as Stanley Kowalski on Broadway when Brando left to do the film version).

In one of his letters from Hollywood, Pancho had urged Johnny not to abandon New Orleans.

"Don't come to California," he warned. "[H]ere in Los Angeles, we are considered peons like we were in Texas. In New Orleans, we live in an international city, and we are treated with respect and good jobs. Both Tenn and I can't wait to get back to work, to be back home."

G.B.

Gregg Barrios received a commission from the Ford Foundation Gateway Program to write *Rancho Pancho*. His *Dark Horse, Pale Rider* about Texas writer Katherine Anne Porter received a CTG-Mark Taper Forum fellowship. His one-man show *I-DJ* was awarded a grant from the Sandra Cisneros Macondo Foundation and its script was published in *Ollantay, the Hispanic Theater Quarterly* in 2008. His forthcoming play *Hard Candy* chronicles the life and times of legendary Texas bad girl Candy Barr. Barrios is a member of the Dramatist Guild and the National Book Critics Circle.